THE LIZARD LIBRARY™

The Bearded Dragon.

Jake Miller

The Rosen Publishing Group's
PowerKids Press™
New York

Published in 2003 by The Rosen Publishing Group, Inc.
29 East 21st Street, New York, NY 10010

First Edition

Editor: Nancy MacDonell Smith
Book Design: Maria E. Melendez

Photo Credits: Cover and title page, p. 15 © Joe McDonald/CORBIS; pp. 4, 11 © Gallo Images/CORBIS; pp. 5, 9, 22 © Michael & Patricia Fogden/CORBIS; p. 7 © O. Alamany & E. Vicens/CORBIS; p. 8 © Frank Lane Picture Agency/CORBIS; p. 17 © David A. Northcott/CORBIS; pp. 12, 13 © M. C. Milligan Photography; p. 14 © A. Root/OSF/Animals Animals; p. 16 © Joe McDonald/Animals Animals; p. 18 © Digital Stock; p. 19 © John Cancallosi/Peter Arnold, Inc.; p. 20 © E. R. Degginger/Animals Animals; all border design lizards © Little Creatures/Digital Vision.

Miller, Jake.
The bearded dragon / Jake Miller.— 1st ed.
     p. cm. — (The lizard library)
Includes bibliographical references (p.   ).
Summary: Brief text describes the appearance, habitat, mating, family life, behavior, and predators of the bearded dragon, a friendly lizard found all over Australia.
   ISBN 0-8239-6412-4 (lib. bdg.)
1. Bearded dragons (Reptiles)—Juvenile literature. [1. Bearded dragons (Reptiles) 2. Lizards.] I. Title. II. Series.
   QL666.L223 M56 2003
   597.95'5—dc21

                                                                    2001006029

Manufactured in the United States of America

Contents

Bearded dragons got their name because they look like they have beards.

A Dragon's Beard

When a bearded dragon puffs up the pouch around the lower part of its **snout**, it is easy to imagine how the lizard gets its name. The pouch has **spikes** that look like a man's beard, and the lizard looks as **fierce** as a dragon. Bearded dragons also have spikes along their sides and near their tails. These make them look even scarier. The truth is, bearded dragons are not as scary as they look. It is true that they are very strong **survivors**. They live in places where few other creatures can **survive**.

A bearded dragon will puff up the pouch around its snout when it wants to frighten an enemy. This makes the bearded dragon seem much bigger and scarier than it really is.

Dragons Everywhere

Bearded dragons are members of a **genus** called Pogona. They are only found in Australia. People all over the world keep them as pets, but Australia is the only place where they live in the wild. The most common **species** is the inland bearded dragon. All the different kinds of bearded dragons have triangle-shaped heads and wide, flat bodies. Inland bearded dragons are the biggest of the bearded dragons. They grow to be about 2 feet (61 cm) long, including their tail. Their bodies are about 10 inches (25 cm) long. Some of the other species, such as the **dwarf** bearded dragon, are half that size. Bearded dragons come in many different colors, from beige and gray to red and bright orange. They are usually the same color as the soil or rocks where they were born. Their color helps them to blend in better with the ground.

This bearded dragon is the same color as the soil. It would be very hard to spot the lizard from a distance.

Baby Dragons

Baby bearded dragons hatch from eggs. When it is time to **breed**, male dragons compete for a **mate** by showing off their beards and nipping other males on the tail. When the female is ready to lay her eggs, she scoops out a nest in the sand and climbs in. Inside the nest, the female bearded dragon lays her eggs. A nest usually has between 10 and 20 eggs. The eggs are white with brown spots. They are about 1 ½ inches (4 cm) long. They aren't hard like chicken eggs. Instead they're soft like leather. When the female finishes laying the eggs, she climbs out of the hole. She covers the eggs with sand and walks away. Once the eggs are in the nest, the parent's job is done. The eggs and the babies that hatch from them are on their own.

A mature male bearded dragon has a head that is very large compared to its body.

When their beards aren't puffed up, bearded dragons look smaller and much less terrifying.

The Cycle of Life

The sun keeps the bearded dragon's eggs warm in their sandy nest. It takes about two months for the eggs to hatch. When the eggs hatch, the baby bearded dragons are about 4 inches (10 cm) long. As soon as they hatch, bearded dragons can take care of themselves. They do not need any help from their parents. They are born ready to catch their own food. They grow very quickly. By the time they are one year old, they are already the same size as adult bearded dragons.

This young female is about two years old and is fully grown. She's ready to start a family of her own.

What's for Dinner? Everything.

Food can be very hard to find in the **harsh** habitat where bearded dragons live. It's lucky that bearded dragons will eat just about anything. They eat all kinds of insects and other animals, such as smaller lizards and small **mammals**. They also eat vegetables, flowers, fruits, greens, and seeds. Baby dragons eat most of the same things that adult dragons do, but babies stick to eating smaller insects instead of trying to eat bigger animals. Bearded dragons can store **nutrients** in their bodies as fat, which helps them to survive when there is no food for them to eat. When food is hard to find, or when

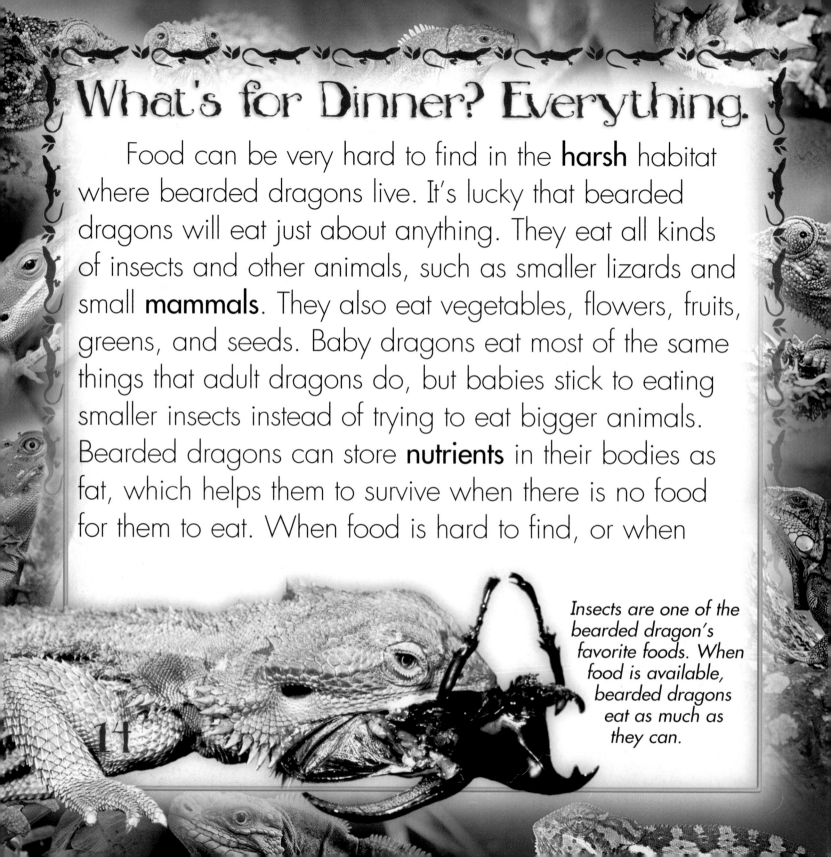

Insects are one of the bearded dragon's favorite foods. When food is available, bearded dragons eat as much as they can.

14

temperatures are too high or too low, bearded dragons become **dormant**. They hide under rocks. They sit very still and wait for the weather to get better. They wait for more food to appear in their habitat.

Though they look scary, bearded dragons are very calm around humans. Sometimes they will even let a human pick them up.

This male is waiting patiently for its prey to come. When an insect or a small animal appears, the bearded dragon will jump on it.

Patient Hunters

Bearded dragons hunt to catch the insects and other animals that they eat. Bearded dragons are "watch and wait" **predators**. This means they find a spot where they can sit very still and wait for their **prey** to appear. When something walks or flies within range, the dragon jumps forward and snaps it up.

One of the bearded dragon's favorite spots to hunt from is on top of a rock or a log. Bearded dragons that live near humans will sometimes perch on top of a fence post or a picnic table to do their hunting.

Though many bearded dragons like to live alone, they will sometimes live in small groups with other bearded dragons.

Hunters Are Hunted, Too

Hunting in broad daylight is a great way to find food, but it also makes bearded dragons targets for other predators. Many different kinds of animals hunt bearded dragons, including birds and snakes. When bearded dragons are frightened by a possible predator, they try to make themselves seem very scary. They flatten their bodies to make themselves look wider. They open their mouths up as wide as they can to make themselves look bigger. They blow up their beards and show off their spikes to try to scare off their enemies. If that doesn't work, bearded dragons will try to run away.

The eagle is one of the animals that preys on the bearded dragon.

Sometimes they stand up on just their back legs to run. It makes them move slower, but they look bigger. A predator might not chase the dragons because they look so big.

This bearded dragon is trying to protect itself by opening its mouth very wide and trying to look bigger than it really is.

How Dragons Communicate

Bearded dragons have many different ways of communicating. They show off their beards to frighten off predators. Puffing up their beards also shows that they are stronger than other dragons. Bearded dragons do push-ups, twitch their tails, and lick each other's heads. They also bob their heads up and down. A strong dragon will bob his head quickly. When a strong lizard bobs its head at a weaker lizard, the weaker lizard answers by waving one of its legs around in a circle. It looks like the weaker dragon is waving hello or is swimming with one arm. Sometimes, instead of waving its arm, the weaker dragon will respond by bobbing its head slowly. If two dragons both bob their heads quickly at each other, they may fight to see who is the strongest.

 This bearded dragon is twitching its tail to show that it is stronger than other dragons.

Beardies as Pets

You don't have to travel to the wilds of Australia to see a bearded dragon. They are one of the most popular kinds of lizards to keep as pets. They are easy to feed and to care for, and they don't grow to be too big to handle. Some bearded dragon owners call their dragons beardies. Beardies are easy to tame, and they like to be around people. They may even learn to perch on their owners' shoulders. They are also fun to watch as they bob their heads, puff up their beards, or hunt for crickets and worms.

The insides of bearded dragons' mouths are usually yellow. This adds to their scary appearance!

Glossary

adapt (uh-DAPT) To change to fit new conditions.

breed (BREED) When a male and female animal get together to have babies.

dormant (DOR-muhnt) Not active. Not moving around, eating, or doing anything at all.

dwarf (DWORF) Plants and animals that are smaller than more common kinds of the same animal.

fierce (FEERS) Brave and dangerous.

genus (JEE-nuhs) The scientific name for a group of similar animals or plants.

habitats (HA-bih-tats) The surroundings where animals or plants live.

harsh (HARSH) Dangerous or difficult.

mammals (MA-mulz) Warm-blooded animals that have backbones and hair, breathe air, and feed milk to their young.

mate (MAYT) A partner for making babies.

nutrients (NOO-tree-ints) Anything a living thing needs for its body to live and to grow.

predators (PREH-duh-terz) Animals that kill other animals for food.

prey (PRAY) An animal that is hunted by another animal for food.

snout (SNOWT) An animal's nose.

species (SPEE-sheez) A single kind of plant or animal. For example, all people are one species.

spikes (SPYKS) Sharp, pointy things shaped like spears or needles.

survive (sur-VYV) To stay alive.

survivors (sur-VY-verz) Things with the ability to stay alive.

temperature (TEM-pruh-chur) How hot or cold something is.

Index

Web Sites

Due to the changing nature of internet links, PowerKids Press has developed an online list of Web sites related to the subject of this book. This site is updated regularly. Please use this link to access the list.

www.powerkidslinks.com/ll/beardrag/